SVABBA CLEAN

Project Manager: Lena Allblom, IKEA FAMILY
Project Leader: Anders Truedsson, IMP Books
Text: Sophie Truedsson, Titel Förlagsbyrå
Layout: thornadvertising.com
International editor and IKEA verbal identity adviser: Janet Colletti, Boco Text
Studio/Boco AB
Fact verification: Eva Jarevik, Chemical Engineer, IKEA FAMILY
Product Campaign & Shop Communication: Anette Json Pihl, IKEA FAMILY
Translation: Comactiva Translations AB, Sweden
Produced by: IMP Books
Printing: Litopat

ISBN 978-91-7417-042-9 (GB)

It's a dirty job, but someone's got to do it.

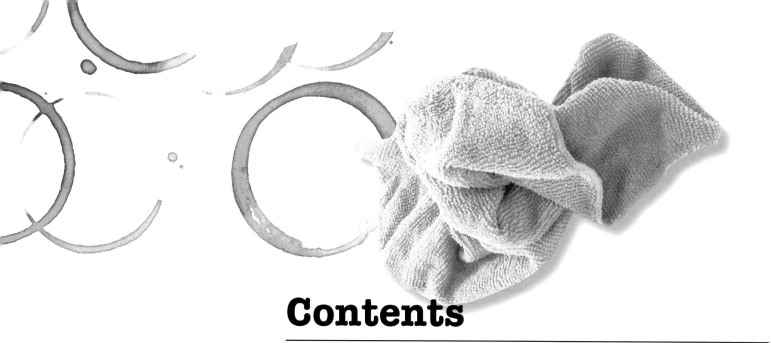

Contents

I came, I saw, I cleaned.

Clean

Cleaning is actually quite simple. Old stains are harder to get rid of than recent ones, and clearing up a bit as you go along makes a big difference. It's true, try it yourself! A cooker hob is actually really easy to wipe off while it's still warm.

This book tells you everything you need to know about smart cleaning. How to get rid of fruit flies, how to clean a floor drain, how to dust methodically. With all these top tips, your everyday life will be practical and efficient – as well as clean and tidy. After all, isn't it great when your home looks nice and clean? When the air smells fresh and you can see the sun shining in through newly cleaned windows?

You can use this book for reference, or read it from cover to cover if you prefer. And you never know when you might need a good cleaning tip, so keep the book handy. On a hook next to the tea-towel, perhaps?

PS. That's why we've attached a fine hanger to the spine.

It's always far better to clean a little and often, than a lot now and then.

A smart home is a great home all week, from Monday to Sunday. Cleaning and washing is always quick and easy, and there's plenty of time left to do other things. To make your home life as easy as you'd like it, you need to create the right conditions. We call it being cleaning-smart. The key is to establish routines and make changes that keep dirt and clutter at bay.

We make cleaning easier by dividing it into three categories: Always, Often and Sometimes. So let's take a journey of cleaning discovery through your home – room by room.

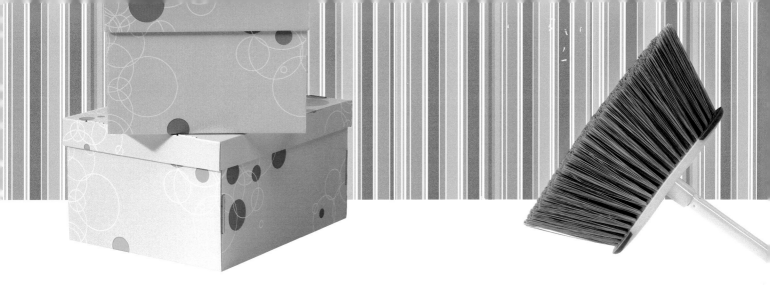

Always

A clean, tidy home – the basics
The secret to a tidy home is called storage. Storage, storage, storage – and clear surfaces! Clear surfaces, of course, are simply an automatic side-effect of good storage. Oh, and one more thing: Think before you hoard! Because at the end of the day, all the storage in the world won't help you if you have 32 different ornamental Santas and endless boxes of stuff you think might come in handy one day.

Plan
Begin by going through your home room by room. What do you want to do in each room, and what things do you need in there? Adapt the storage accordingly. Write a list, and focus on one room at a time.

Furniture
Some items of furniture are easier to clean than others. High legs make it easier to get underneath with the vacuum cleaner. Closed cabinets and shelving units keep dust away and mean there are fewer little ornaments to dust. Cables are dust magnets as well. Have as few cables as possible on the floor, and clip them to the skirting boards, beading or under furniture.

Storage
Whichever room you're working on, think storage. There are all kinds of good-looking boxes and storage baskets, and mixing open and closed storage is a good way of creating effect. Mark each box with a clear label: bills, magazines, hairclips, building blocks. Everything should have a place, and there's nothing to stop it being fun either!

Cleaning routine Establish cleaning routines around the house, like taking your shoes off as soon as you walk in, or everyone helping clear away the breakfast things. If there are many of you in the family, split the housework up into different areas of responsibility, or draw up a roster. It may feel like taking it all a bit too seriously, but give it a go. You won't believe how much easier it makes everything. If everyone clears up after themselves, you've already come a long way. After all, we're the ones who make the mess, and no one else.

Equipment Invest in some decent cleaning equipment, and keep it readily accessible so it's there when you need it.

Often

Things you can do almost every day

The things that need doing often are easy to sneak into your everyday life, such as general tidying and wiping. Why not sort out the papers while you're on the phone, or scrub the sink while you're waiting for the kettle to boil? Deal with the problem before it grows into a bigger one. All jobs are quick if you keep on top of them.

Air The best way to freshen up around the house is to open some windows. Air the bedroom first thing in the morning and scare away unpleasant mites. Once a week, treat your home to a full-blown airing with a through-draught.

Declutter Give or throw away things you don't use. And even if retail therapy's your thing, try to think before you buy: don't buy new until the old stuff's run out. Try to stick to the "one in, one out" principle. After all, the fewer things you have at home, the easier it is to keep it uncluttered.

Pick up Clear up after yourself. Pick things up as soon as you've finished with them. For big families, teamwork is the key. Make sure everyone is responsible for their own bits and pieces. Teach the smaller family members that there's a place for everything. Have a few minutes' tidying-up time just before bedtime every day.

Dust Vacuum clean the whole house once a week. Prevent dirt from spreading by giving the kitchen, hallway and bathroom an extra run-round with the vacuum. Dust surfaces with a damp cloth as required.

Wipe Mop the floor in the rooms that are used most, and scrub or wipe bathroom and kitchen furniture and fittings.

Older stains
are harder to
get rid of than
recent ones...

Sometimes

Those extra jobs that only need doing occasionally
Some cleaning only needs to be done once or twice a year. And if you're good at keeping on top of things, those big cleaning jobs will be that much easier. Oh – and another thing: you don't have to spring clean the entire house in one go. You can do one thing at a time. Air the bed linen one day, defrost the freezer another. You're still doing a big clean, just not all at once.

Dust Wipe furniture with a damp cloth – ideally of the miracle cloth type made of synthetic microfibre. Vacuum sofas, armchairs and beds.

Wipe Mop all hard floors in bedrooms and the living room. Wipe and clean interiors such as cabinet doors, ornaments, ventilation fans and doors. Take particular care in the kitchen and bathroom. Clean the windows.

Spring cleaning Some people think the occasional big spring clean is a must, but we disagree. The secret is groundwork. If you keep on top of things by cleaning regularly, your home will never become chaotically untidy. If you really want to spring clean, go ahead! Otherwise, systematic cleaning is enough.

How?

This section contains some useful tips on how to clean all your home's nooks and crannies quickly and easily. Are you really using all the functions on your vacuum cleaner? And how do you unblock a sink? Cleaning is astoundingly easy when you know how.

Clean in the right order Open up the windows to air your home. Begin by cleaning and wiping in the bathroom and kitchen, and then move on to the rest of the house. Finish off by vacuuming and mopping the floors.

Dust Dust using a damp miracle cloth and add a little diluted soft soap if required. Use separate cloths for the bathroom, kitchen and living room, and you'll avoid spreading so many germs. Methodical dusting saves time. Think from high to low – start with the top shelves and work down. That way you'll catch the dust that falls down onto lower surfaces. Establish a dusting round and always dust your home in the same order. A little routine will make it all go much faster.

It takes longer to think about vacuuming for three days than it does to simply get it done.

Clean the windows Start by clearing windowsills of plants, lamps and other items. Fill a bucket with lukewarm water and a little washing-up liquid. Use a dishcloth or sponge to wet the window. Wash hard enough to remove dirt. Wipe the top of the window frame with a terry towel or cotton cloth to prevent water running down and making streaks. Then dry the window using a squeegee. Finish off by drying the frame. Don't be tempted to give the window another wipe, it will only leave streaks.

Vacuum You probably already know how to vacuum, but there's no harm in running through some of the vacuum cleaner's excellent functions. The various attachments open up a whole world of opportunities.

The standard floor tool has two settings, brush in or brush out. The brush should be out for flooring and other hard surfaces, and in for rugs and wall-to-wall carpets.

The dust brush can be used as a dust cloth and is ideal for dusting books and bookcases, as well as lamp shades and pictures.

The crevice tool is great for getting behind radiators and into awkward spots on upholstered furniture.

The upholstery tool is for sofas, beds and other fabrics.

Tip: Put a nylon stocking over the nozzle to vacuum inside drawers, for example, and avoid sucking up the wrong things.

Mop floors Mopping or swabbing entails cleaning the floors with water. One common error, however, is to use far too much water – having a small lake in your home isn't good for the floor, or for dirt. Squeeze the mop an extra time, and don't use too much detergent.

Wood Oil-treated wooden floors may be sensitive to water and detergents. Take care and use a well wrung-out mop and a sparing amount of soft soap, approximately one capful (10 ml) per litre of water. Parquet and varnished wooden floors should be cleaned with a well wrung-out mop and a sparing amount of soft soap, around half a capful (5 ml) per litre of water.

Stone Don't use strong detergents as they may dissolve joints and ruin the floor. Wash with a wrung-out mop and soft soap, one capful (10 ml) per litre of water.

Vinyl, laminate and linoleum The water shouldn't be too hot. Use a wrung-out mop and soft soap, around half a capful (5 ml) per litre of water.

What you need

Have you decided to chase those dust balls away? Good! But don't forget to make sure your cleaning cupboard is fully equipped before you get started. When was the last time you splashed out on a decent mop and cleaning cloths? Design and function will lift your cleaning to new heights, making it not only simpler but lots more fun. And it's really annoying having to stop in the middle of everything just because there's something missing.

Vacuum cleaner Pretty much a must in any cleaning cupboard. If you have a big house on more than one floor, you might like to have a vacuum cleaner on each floor. There are also small rechargeable ones for clearing up crumbs from the kitchen worktop.

Dustpan and brush/broom A dustpan and brush – or even better the long variety with a short broom – means you don't have to get the vacuum out and can sweep up dirt and spillages before they spread.

Mop and wringer Mops made of microfibre make the floor less wet.

Bucket It's worth having several sizes of bucket, at least one big one and one small one. Try to find one in a nice colour and bring a little everyday luxury to your cleaning!

Cloths Have at least three microfibre miracle cloths, ideally in different colours – one for the kitchen, one for the bathroom and one for the living room. You'll also need something for the window frames when you're cleaning the windows. A terry cloth or a standard cotton cloth are both okay, as long as they are lint-free.

Miracle cloths are cloths made of synthetic microfibre.

They remove dirt and bacteria without detergent. Once the cloths get dirty you can machine wash them to make them like new again.

Dishwashing sponges
Sponges are available with different grades of scourer. Take care with the scouring side as it can easily scratch delicate sink units and tiles. Sponges can be washed in the dishwasher and used again.

Squeegee
Cleaning windows is faster with a squeegee, and good ones will have a replaceable rubber strip. Rubber is perishable, and it may be hard to get your windows properly clean if the strip dries out. You can also get floor squeegees for wetroom floors, although they tend to have rounded edges.

Toilet brush
For the inside of the toilet bowl.

Washing-up brushes
One for the washing-up, one for the bathroom sink and one for the toilet. Just be sure to keep them separate!

Toothbrush
Save your old toothbrushes! They're great for cleaning in confined spaces and recesses.

SOFT SOAP – Pine fresh
Ditch the synthetic chemicals in your cleaning cupboard – the new SVABBA soft soap will do all your dirty work. This multipurpose cleaner is made from purest pine oil from the Swedish forests, tackling grease and grime the natural way. You can use it to clean your oven, remove stains from clothes, even to prevent pests in the garden – all while it's reducing the load on the environment.

Soft soap An old, tried and tested cleaning agent, soft soap may seem old-fashioned but it's pretty much all you need. It's effective and doesn't contain all the unnecessary chemicals found in many modern detergents.

Diluted soft soap

• 1 tbsp soft soap

• 750 ml water

• Mix and pour into a spray bottle

Washing-up liquid Not just for washing-up! Washing-up liquid dissolves grease and is effective on hard dirt stains. A liquid with a neutral pH is mild and can be used on any surface that can cope with water. Prolonged contact may dry your skin, so use rubber gloves.

Vinegar and citric acid/lemon juice

Vinegar – the white distilled kind – removes bad smells and ingrained stains. Citric acid or lemon juice is often used in cooking, but it's also good for lime and rust marks in toilets, wash-basins and bathtubs. Wear rubber gloves when using powdered citric acid.

Spray bottles Fill spray bottles with diluted soft soap and keep them where you think they'll be needed. The kitchen, the bathroom – you know best!

Apron Carry your cleaning things around in your apron pocket and they're always at hand. A large pocket is great for storing all the things you find as you work – cleaning always turns up a few coins, pens or hairgrips.

Storage box A cleaning box with compartments is very handy for storing cleaning products. There's a place for everything – even in the cleaning box!

Kitchen

MEMO

- Does your wooden chopping board smell bad? Pour plenty of table salt directly onto the board and rub in lightly with a damp cloth. Then rinse it with hot water and washing-up liquid.

- Don't forget to clean behind the waste bin in the kitchen. All kinds of nasty surprises could be lurking there.

- A dustpan and brush/broom is the best way to clear up crumbs and spillages in the kitchen. Keep one close by.

- For an extra shiny sink and draining board, pour on cold water and wipe dry immediately. Et voilà!

Everyone loves the kitchen

The kitchen is the heart of the home. A place for cooking, baking, tasting and making a mess. And they do say the quickest way to the heart is through the stomach. The kitchen is a place for intimate conversation, where everyday problems are aired. Parts of our lives are played out over steaming pots and potato peelings.

But humans aren't the only ones who love the kitchen – germs thrive among the food and mess here! A kitchen is a veritable smorgasbord of grease, breadcrumbs and moisture. And if you don't want uninvited guests, keeping it clean is definitely the way to go!

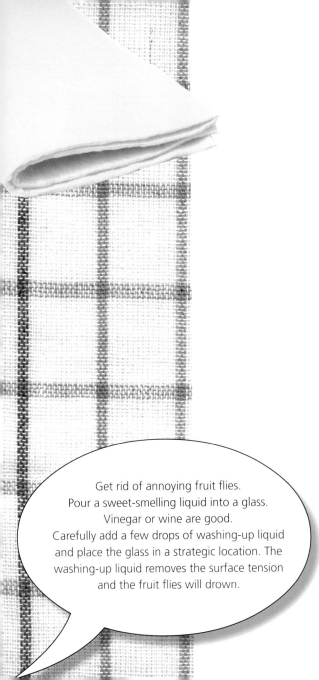

Always in the kitchen

It's easy to be blind to shortcomings in your own kitchen, so try to look at it as if it were someone else's. Is it easy to find what you need? Is your kitchen well planned? Avoid unnecessary running around and mess by dividing your kitchen into different areas of use.

Keep utensils where they're easy to find, but avoid having too much stuff out on the worktop. Keep spatulas and the like in a drawer near the cooker. Keep sponges and detergents easily accessible under the sink.

Don't have too many rugs and fabrics.

A dishwasher may be a good investment. You'll avoid arguments about whose turn it is to do the washing-up, your dishes will be cleaner and the worktops will be clear of dirty things. Many modern dishwashers are also environmentally friendly.

Only use the dishcloth on the sink, draining board, worktops and cooker, never on chopping boards or floors. A dirty dish-cloth is one of the worst germ spreaders in the kitchen.

Keep a dustpan and brush/broom close by – that way it's easy to sweep up crumbs before they start spreading.

Get rid of annoying fruit flies.
Pour a sweet-smelling liquid into a glass.
Vinegar or wine are good.
Carefully add a few drops of washing-up liquid and place the glass in a strategic location. The washing-up liquid removes the surface tension and the fruit flies will drown.

Often in the kitchen

Clear out the fridge – old food takes up space unnecessarily and can also turn into germ bombs.

Always wash up immediately after cooking or eating – it's quicker and easier that way.

Ideally, vacuum clean the kitchen floor twice a week.

Wipe the cooker directly after use. The sink too.

The kitchen floor will stay clean and fresh if you mop it once a week. Obviously this varies depending on the number of people in your household. If you live alone, every other week will probably be enough.

Change the tea-towel and dishcloth. Dishcloths can be washed in the dishwasher or washing machine and reused.

Empty the rubbish.

Sometimes in the kitchen

Clean the cooker and microwave. Most ovens have wheels at the back to make it easier to pull them out so you can clean behind them.

Defrost the fridge and freezer, and wipe the inside. Use washing-up liquid or diluted soft soap.

The cooker hood and filters need cleaning occasionally, depending on how much and how often you cook.

Clean the tiles and take particular care around the cooker.

Wipe drawers and other dry areas, both inside and out.

How?

Kitchen unit doors Believe it or not, but the best way to wash kitchen unit doors is from the bottom up, and then down again. That way you avoid dirt streaks.

Sink unit Stainless steel units should be cleaned with washing-up liquid – use a miracle cloth or a kitchen sponge. The sink needs a bit of extra effort. Wash it thoroughly with washing-up liquid, or use a coarse brush and soft soap.

Cooker Electric hobs with black plates are best cleaned with a sponge and diluted soft soap. And remember, cleaning is easier when the hob is still a bit warm.

Hobs made from ceramic glass look nice, but they scratch easily. Never use steel wool or knives when removing spots and stains. Ideally, remove the stains with the soft side of a sponge while the hob is still warm. If something more drastic is needed, however, scrape the stains off with a razor blade. Finish off by buffing with a dry cloth.

The oven should be cleaned using a miracle cloth and soft soap. In case of severe soiling, start by giving it a rough clean, spraying it with equal parts soft soap and water. Then switch the oven on to 100°C for about 10 minutes, and give it a good wipe once cooled.

Cooker hood Many hood filters can be washed in the dishwasher. Alternatively, soak the filter in water mixed with a small amount of soft soap and washing-up liquid.

Tiles Clean using a dishwashing sponge moistened with lukewarm water and washing-up liquid. Use the soft side of the sponge. The scouring pad can scratch the tiles, allowing dirt and grease to stick more easily.

Fridge and freezer Freezers must be defrosted unless you have a self-defrosting model. The inside of the fridge should be cleaned a couple of times a year. Take out all the food and wipe with a cloth and diluted soft soap. Also wipe jars, containers and packets before putting them back in. Rubbing a little white vinegar on the rubber strip in the door helps prevent mould.

Microwave
Here's a great tip for cleaning a microwave oven: Put a bowl of water in the microwave and heat until boiling point. Let the water steam for a minute or so, then simply wipe the inside of the microwave. If it's heavily soiled, try adding two teaspoons of white vinegar to the water.

Coffee filter machine
Remove lime scale deposits by mixing 200 ml of vinegar with 800 ml of water. Then brew the mixture through the machine a couple of times. Finally, run the brew cycle once again using clean water only.

Wash your hands! Always wash your hands before handling food.

Living room

MEMO

- Bad smells? A bowl of vinegar will absorb smells and cleanse the air.

- Prolong the enjoyment. Cold water and a teaspoon of baking powder makes tulips last longer.

- Have you been dancing in the living room? Scuff marks on the floor can be removed using an ordinary pencil eraser.

A new room every day

A living room can be used for just about anything. Painting, dancing, reading, singing, relaxing, playing games, doing somersaults – literally anything! Every day the living room can be something different and exciting, or it can just be nice and cosy. A great place to relax and spend time together.

Spend a little extra time and energy when planning your living room. Choose storage that genuinely suits your needs. After all, there has to be room for all that fun. So how about it? Home cinema or circus ring? What will your living room be today?

Always in the living room

Think function: what do you want to do in your living room, and what do you need?

Choose furniture that's easy to care for. A sofa with removable, washable covers will withstand some mess and spillage, and leather is generally easy to wipe off.

Choose ornaments carefully, and have only the nicest ones on show.

Only have as many pot plants as you have time to look after.

Keep your DVD player and games console in a TV cabinet where they won't gather as much dust. Clip cables to the skirting boards or beading to avoid having them in a messy tangle on the floor.

Keep CDs and DVDs in closed boxes or drawers.

Often in the living room

Vacuum as part of your weekly cleaning routine.

Dust – the TV in particular attracts a lot of dust.

Pick up unnecessary things that are lying around making the room look untidy.

Puff up the cushions on the sofa. Isn't it amazing how something so little can make such a difference?

Water the plants.

Sometimes in the living room

Wipe chairs and other furniture with a damp miracle cloth.

Tidy the sofa. If you're lucky you'll find some coins for your piggy bank.

Clean, tidy and sort the bookshelves.

Wipe the skirting boards, beading and plug sockets with a miracle cloth.

Mist your pot plants, either using a spray bottle or by putting them under the shower.

Mop any hard floors.

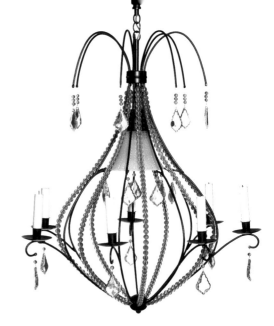

How?

Pick up Put each remote control on top of the machine it belongs to, old newspapers and magazines in the recycling pile and CDs back in their cases. Fold blankets and puff up cushions – and hey presto, your living room's tidy!

Sofa Take the seating cushions outside and beat them with a carpet beater. Vacuum all surfaces and nooks with the upholstery tool attachment. Wash the removable covers if applicable. Leather sofas should be wiped with a damp cloth.

TV and music system Wipe using a miracle cloth. Mixing a small amount of fabric softener into the water has an antistatic effect and will stop dust coming straight back again.

Cut-glass chandeliers Switch off the power. Use a sturdy ladder and hang an open umbrella below the chandelier. This will collect water and stop glass drops from falling on the floor. Clean with a cloth dipped in lukewarm water mixed with washing-up liquid, then wipe using a dry cloth.

Bookcases Take all the books out and dust them using the dust brush attachment on the vacuum cleaner. Wipe the shelves using a damp miracle cloth and diluted soft soap.

Sorting your books by the colour of their spine can turn your bookcase into a small work of art.

Bedroom

MEMO

- Don't have too much clutter on bedside tables.

- Venetian blinds can be awkward to clean, but if you put on a pair of soft cotton gloves and wet the fingers in soapy water, it's easier to reach the dust.

- Remember to think lofty thoughts when you're dusting – work from the top down!

Do not disturb, relaxation in progress

Sleep is a wonderful thing, and there's nothing quite like snuggling down between newly laundered sheets. That lovely clean feeling, and the sweet smell of fresh bed linen. As you slip away into sleep, your thoughts fly off and nothing should be allowed to disturb you. Hustle and bustle can stay on the sofa – the bedroom is a place for peace and quiet. Sleep well, and in the morning open your eyes to a brand new day.

Always in the bedroom

High legs on a bed make it easier to get underneath with the vacuum cleaner. It's also a way of making space for more storage: there are large boxes with castors and handles that are ideal for under-bed storage.

Having a balcony off the bedroom isn't only a luxury, it's also very practical – you can let fresh air in or hang out your bedclothes to air.

Use chests of drawers and fitted/freestanding wardrobes to store your clothes out of sight – it makes for a greater sense of calm in the bedroom.

A small laundry basket in the bedroom is great for socks and dirty clothes that otherwise tend to end up on the floor.

Often in the bedroom

Airing is a great, simple way to keep your bedroom fresh and free of dust and mites. Open the window for a while in the morning before you make the bed.

Keep it tidy. Clean clothes should go in drawers and wardrobes, dirty clothes in a laundry basket.

Change bedclothes regularly.

Dust windowsills and any shelves. There's a lot of fabric in a bedroom, so it quickly becomes dusty.

Sometimes in the bedroom

Take all bedclothes outside to air and beat them. Take this opportunity to vacuum the headboard.

Turn the mattress occasionally to keep it fresh and firm for longer.

Clean the venetian blinds – assuming they're not fitted between double-glazed windows.

Mop the floors as necessary.

Wash any rugs that look dirty.

How?

Venetian blinds Wipe with a damp miracle cloth, or use the dust brush attachment on your vacuum cleaner.

Bed Vacuum the mattress with the upholstery tool, and wipe the headboard with a damp miracle cloth.

Bedclothes Down pillows become like new if they're machine washed and tumble dried. Wash pillows at 60°C and spin, then tumble dry on a long cycle.

Down quilts can be machine washed, although you'll need a large machine that can take 5 kg. Follow the washing instructions.

Tip: Sew the pillow into a pillowcase before washing, just in case a seam should split. Tumble dry down pillows with two tennis balls to make them extra fluffy.

Wall-to-wall carpets Vacuum clean with the standard floor tool, with the brush pulled in. All carpets need cleaning now and then – call a professional for help and advice. Special carpet cleaning machines are available to hire.

Rugs Most rag-rugs are machine washable. Or scrub the rug using a scrubbing brush and soft soap, and then rinse. This should be done outdoors.

Jewellery A quick way to polish silver jewellery:

You will need water, aluminium foil, baking powder (2 tsp/litre of water), salt (2 tsp/litre of water).

Line the bottom of a bowl with aluminium foil and place your jewellery on top. Sprinkle with baking powder and salt, and then pour boiling water over the silver. It will bubble and hiss a fair bit, but that's okay. Wait until the bubbling stops, then remove the silver. Wash the pieces in water and dry with a towel.

Gilded jewellery must not be polished in this way as it may remove the gilt. Never polish gilded areas, they should only be wiped.

Keep your jewellery in an attractive case –
it can be your very own treasure chest.

Bathroom

MEMO

- Clean and shiny! Add an extra shine to your wash-basin and bathtub by buffing with a dry cloth after cleaning.

- Get rid of brown stains. Running water can leave unsightly streaks and rust spots on ceramic surfaces in bathrooms, but citric acid is the solution. Moisten a sponge and sprinkle on a little citric acid, rub onto discoloured areas and leave to soak a good while. Next, scrub using diluted soft soap and a brush. Finally, rinse thoroughly.

- Take care of your hands! Wear rubber gloves when using citric acid.

The cleanest room

A revitalising shower in the morning, or a relaxing bath in the evening? Whichever you prefer, the bathroom is where we make ourselves nice and clean. Our most private and intimate room – but also one of the most highly frequented.

The bathroom rush hour starts early in the morning, and tends to carry on till the evening. And if you haven't got room to swing a cat, the key is to be smart. Functional bathroom cabinets and generous towel shelves make a biiig difference.

Always in the bathroom

Wall-hung furniture keeps floor space free and makes it easier to mop. If you're renovating, try to find a toilet with as few angles and crannies as possible, as they're easier to keep clean.

Don't skimp on storage. Large bathroom cabinets with doors keep dirt out and things in.

Store cleaning supplies close at hand. Keep brushes, sponges and diluted soft soap under the sink, so it's easy to get them out and clean when the fancy takes you.

Underfloor heating will quickly dry wet floors. If you use a bath mat, choose one that's machine washable.

Hang a lot of hooks and invest in a towel dryer. That way, you'll avoid having wet towels lying around on the floor.

Mix business with pleasure. A comfy stool is perfect for quiet times, and if there's storage under the seat it's ideal for laundry.

Dry off. Let the bathroom dry out after you've used it. Leave the door open, switch on the fan or open a window.

Help each other! If everyone takes responsibility and cleans up after themselves, the bathroom will stay fresh for a long time.

Often in the bathroom

The wash-basin and toilet should be cleaned at least once a week. And while you're at it, why not tackle the bath or shower as well?

Throw away any old, half-empty shampoo bottles and crumbly soaps; they're not worth saving.

Empty the waste bin often.

Mop the bathroom floor weekly, it gets dirty quickly. Silverfish love dirty bathrooms – they feast on hair and skin flakes!

Wash the bath mat as often as you can. It attracts both moisture and dirt, which isn't a great combination.

Polish the bathroom mirror.

Change the towels.

Sometimes in the bathroom

Move everything out of the bathroom and give it a thorough clean. Clean the floors, walls and ceiling. Wipe all bottles, jars and pots before you put them back in their place.

Clean the floor drain (if you have a wetroom). Unpleasant smells in the bathroom may come from old dirt that's gathered in the drain.

Clean under the bath if you have a freestanding tub, removing any panels to ensure the best access.

Unexpected guests? If you only have time to clean one room, make sure it's the bathroom – they're bound to visit it at least once.

How?

Tiles Clean floor and wall tiles with washing-up liquid and a sponge. Tough lime deposits can be treated with citric acid/lemon juice on a damp sponge. Rub it in and leave to soak a while before wiping it off again. Then rinse. Take care of your hands! Wear rubber gloves.

Wash-basin The more often you clean the sink, the easier it is. Use a washing-up brush and diluted soft soap. Awkward spots and the areas around the taps are easiest to access with a toothbrush. Finish off by buffing with a dry cloth for added shine.

Blocked pipes! Hair, grease and soap residue can coagulate and block your pipes. The best way to deal with the problem is to unscrew the pipes and clean out the water trap by hand.

Toilet Remove the seat and rinse it in the bath or shower, then clean with diluted soft soap and a sponge. The outside of the toilet bowl and cistern should be cleaned with a washing-up brush and the diluted soft soap. For the inside, use a toilet brush. Mix a few tablespoons of white vinegar with soft soap and pour into the bowl. Leave it to stand a while before scrubbing the bowl and flushing.

Psst! Dirt tends to gather underneath the toilet rim where you can't see it. The best tool for reaching it is a washing-up brush.

Bathtub
Rinse and wipe the tub straight after a bath. This will prevent ingrained deposits and the dirt will run off easily. Keep a bottle of diluted soft soap and a bath brush nearby.

If you have a freestanding tub, old soap, water and skin deposits tend to gather underneath. Remove any panels and clean as much as you can by showering the area. For the rest, use a long-handled brush and soft soap.

Floor
Mop the floor with a wrung-out mop and soft soap.

Slipping hazard! Mopped vinyl floors can be extremely slippery. Reduce the risk by mopping a second time with clean water and then wiping with a dry cloth.

Floor drain
If you have a wetroom with an open floor drain, remove the grate and scrub it with soft soap, taking care to rinse thoroughly afterwards. Clear the open drain by hand – rubber gloves recommended. Scrub round the edges and rinse with hot water.

Shower curtain
Spray the shower curtain with diluted soft soap after showering to avoid deposits. Some shower curtains can be machine washed – check the washing instructions.

Mirror
Use a wet miracle cloth to remove spots, then wipe with a dry cloth. Polishing the bathroom mirror with shaving foam and drying with lint-free paper will prevent the glass steaming up.

Children's room

MEMO

- Let your children have a say in how their room is decorated and furnished. Cleaning's much more fun if you like the way the room looks.

- Necklaces should be in the treasure chest, and the puppet lives in the drawer. Make tidying-up a natural part of play – use plenty of fun, practical storage.

- Giving your children their own laundry basket is an easy way of making sure dirty clothes don't just get thrown on the floor.

- Every now and again, let chaos reign – children's rooms should be like that sometimes.

A fantasy room

When kids are left to their own devices, anything can happen. The blanket becomes a magic king's robe, the bed a magnificent castle. Toys take on a life of their own, and somehow they fly out all over the floor – all by themselves!

Luckily, tidying up never takes that long. And a mess is pretty inevitable when all that fun's being had. The difficult thing is finding a good home for all those cars, dolls, skipping ropes and crayons. After all, there should be a place for everything.

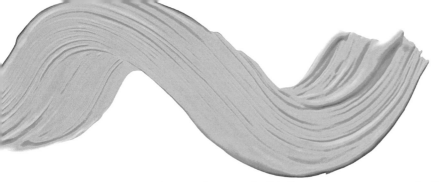

Always in the children's room

Think low. Hang children's clothes so they can reach them themselves. In a children's room, storage and shelving should be adapted to the children's height.

Make sure there are plenty of big boxes and storage baskets. Label them with fun, silly drawings. Cars on the car box, crayons on the colouring box – draw them yourselves or cut pictures out of magazines. Let the kids choose the colour of their storage boxes.

A box under the bed will take loads of toys. One with castors and a lid is handy and can easily be pushed around the room.

See-through boxes make it easier to find and remember things. Now where did I put that toy?

Hooks are great for just about everything: skipping ropes, PE bags and school bags.

Have a few minutes' tidying-up time every evening. In fact, why not make it into a fun game? See who can pick up the most toys in the shortest time!

Avoid delicate rugs and fabrics that damage easily.

Often in the children's room

Wash up the toy tea set – kids can have people round for coffee several times a week.

Vacuum – all that playing, jumping and bouncing causes a lot of dust.

Dust and wipe all surfaces with a miracle cloth and diluted soft soap.

Sometimes in the children's room

Many soft toys can be machine washed. If not, try a mild hand-wash or hang them out to air.

Clear out old toys, and sell or donate any that aren't used any more.

How?

Wall Have the kids been drawing on the walls again? Crayon marks can be removed with toothpaste on a cloth. Rub the mark until it comes off, then wash the area with a damp miracle cloth.

Toys Avoid strong chemicals. Clean toys with a miracle cloth and lukewarm water. Use a little washing-up liquid if necessary.

Children's hands Paint-covered hands can be washed with soap and lukewarm water.

Extra-tough soap bubbles that can be absolutely gigantic.

400 ml water
100 ml washing-up liquid
50 ml glycerine
½ tsp granulated sugar

Mix the water and sugar thoroughly. Add the glycerine and washing-up liquid. Ready to go!

Hallway

MEMO

- Child-friendly homes have coat hooks a bit lower down. That way, children can reach and put away their own outdoor clothes.

- A place for keys just inside the door can save the absent-minded person a lot of time.

- Shoes are happiest when they're polished, and clothes are happiest on hangers.

- Quick-dry wellies with a hairdryer.

Hi, welcome home!

The hallway is the first thing we see when we come in the door, and that first impression is all-important. We need this taking-off zone to be neat and tidy. So there's only one real solution: to get as much as possible into the smallest possible amount of space.

After all, is there anything more annoying when you're in a rush than looking for things that have vanished into thin air? And how nice is it to stumble over piles of shoes and coats? When everything is in its own place, it's easy to find things – and easy to feel welcome.

Always in the hallway

Stop dirt at the door. Have a shoe-scraper or grid outside the front door, and a decent doormat just inside.

Plenty of storage. Screen off clothes with wardrobes, sliding doors or a fabric drape. This will make the hall look tidier, and there'll also be less dust.

A good shoe rack keeps shoes in one place and makes vacuuming easier.

Put up hooks for bags and a hat shelf for cycle helmets and other headgear.

What is it that tends to end up in the hallway? Post, mobile phones, keys, sunglasses. Just accept that this kind of thing will always be in the hallway, and give them a smart place to stay instead. How about an attractive bowl or a key cabinet?

A well-organised hallway works, even on stressful days. A mirror just by the door could be handy. That way you avoid having to walk in with shoes on for that last check in the mirror.

Often in the hallway

Declutter! Give or throw away old shoes and clothes you no longer use. Don't have too many pairs of shoes out – put them in the wardrobe.

Vacuum a couple of times a week – you're not the only ones who use the front door. Grit and gravel come in this way, too!

In snowy and slushy weather, ideally mop the hall floor once a week.

Sometimes in the hallway

Shake and air the hall rug.

Hang clothes out to air.

Swap outdoor clothes around depending on the season. During the summer you can put winter clothes away, and vice versa.

How?

Clothes Air your clothes regularly to avoid mites and unpleasant smells. Empty the pockets and do up zips and buttons if you're hanging the clothes away for a long time. That helps them keep their shape better.

Floor Taking your shoes off as soon as you come in is a good habit to get into. It makes cleaning easier and puts less strain on the floor. Use a broom to sweep up dirt and grit before it spreads.

Shoes Even shoes have to rest occasionally. Don't use the same pair more than one day in a row. Fresh air and shoe trees help shoes keep their shape. Wet shoes will dry faster if you stuff them with newspaper.

Leather shoes keep longer if you polish them regularly. Begin by removing dirt and dust with a damp cloth. Then rub in a suitable colour of shoe polish or cream, and leave to stand a while. Finish off by buffing with a soft cloth. Remember to treat leather shoes and boots using a suitable spray or cream. Wet leather shoes should dry at room temperature. Drying on or near a radiator ruins the leather.

Textile shoes with a rubber sole can often be machine washed and tumble dried. Otherwise, try lukewarm water and soap. A waterproofing spray will protect them against dirt and moisture.

Suede shoes are sensitive and best cleaned with a suede cleaning brush. Stains can be removed using a special suede cleaner, and the colour can be revitalised using a suede spray. Suede treatment is a must.

Workspace

MEMO

- Put castors on your furniture to make vacuuming easier.

- A little colour in the workspace works wonders. How about a nice flowering plant or a picture?

- A whiteboard or noticeboard is always handy for kids' drawings, invitations and reminders.

Like at work – but homely

A desk in the home workspace is a mixture of business and pleasure. There has to be room for bills and felt-tip pens, and it's nice to have a separate place for general pottering. A place where it's okay to leave out the sewing machine and the odd half-finished project. But ideally, it should also be possible to shut the door occasionally for those times when you really need to concentrate.

Just watch out for those dust balls! They love a workspace – and all those piles of tangled cables.

Always in the workspace

Function, function, function. Sewing, painting, or just sitting at the computer? Think about what you want to use the room for, and plan from there.

Adapt the storage accordingly. Ideally, everyone in the family should have their own drawer or drawer unit.

Use cable trunking or clip loose cables up somewhere, otherwise those dust balls will get all caught up in the tangles.

Have a system for incoming bills, post, newspapers and magazines. Use a variety of boxes, magazine racks and folders.

Mark storage units with labels, or use see-through boxes. That way, everyone knows where things should be and they'll be easier to find.

Plan for a mess. It's more fun to paint and glue when you know it won't take long to clear it all away. One good idea is to have a wax tablecloth or a large sheet handy.

Often in the workspace

Sort post and bills. Put the bills in folders as you pay them, and discard or donate old newspapers and magazines.

Clear and reorganise your desk regularly. Keep one pile as a kind of inbox and deal with papers as they come in.

Vacuum as part of your weekly cleaning routine.

Wipe down the computer.

Dust all surfaces, not forgetting lamp shades and pictures.

Sometimes in the workspace

Wipe the skirting boards, beading, light switches and plug sockets.

Tidy the desk drawers.

How?

Skirting boards and beading Clean
using hot water and a mixture of washing-up liquid and
soft soap. An old toothbrush is good for those awkward
places.

Computer Switch off the computer before wiping
it clean. Vacuum the keyboard or turn it upside down.
Use a cotton bud to get between the keys. Use water
mixed with a little washing-up liquid, but never spray
water directly on the computer. Always check any special
instructions in the computer's user manual.

Wardrobe

MEMO

- Having all the same clothes hangers makes a wardrobe that bit more luxurious.

- A little nostalgia never hurt anyone. If you want to save something for the kids or grandchildren, buy quality clothes.

- Carpet beetles are nasty little creatures that like to set up home in the wardrobe and eat holes in our clothes. But they hate being disturbed, so move stuff around frequently and let in plenty of light.

- Put a dry bar of soap in your underwear drawer. It smells lovely!

A place for favourites

We all dream of a large wardrobe with plenty of storage space. Clothes hanging nicely and neatly, preferably arranged into colour categories. And perhaps an armchair as well, somewhere to sit and ponder what trousers to wear today.

But a small wardrobe can be functional as well, and surely having too many clothes is just too much mess and hard work anyway. At the end of the day, the best thing is a perfectly semi-messy wardrobe containing just your favourites.

Always in the wardrobe

Go through your wardrobe carefully and decide what you really need. Do you have a lot of shirts? Then you need long clothes racks with plenty of room for hangers.

Mix hanging and folded storage. Divide the wardrobe with a lot of shelves to avoid large piles of clothes.

Clothes you use often should be easy to get out and put away again.

Keep shoes on a shoe rack or in shoeboxes. Label the boxes or take photos and stick them on. A nice, simple way to keep things organised.

Put lids on boxes that aren't used daily to keep out dirt and dust.

Hooks are always handy for hanging up belts, bags, dressing gowns and jewellery.

Good lighting makes finding things easier. There are basic battery lamps that are inexpensive to buy if your wardrobe doesn't have electric lights.

Often in the wardrobe

Put clean washing away neatly. If you don't have time to do so immediately, it's better to wait and do it properly later.

One in, one out. Discard old underwear and T-shirts every time you buy new ones.

Sometimes in the wardrobe

Discard and donate! Clothes that haven't been worn for several years won't be worn in the future either. Go through your clothes regularly.

Mend holes and sew on buttons, otherwise the garments will just be left lying there – it'll only take a minute.

Empty the whole wardrobe and hang the clothes out to air. Wipe the shelves using a miracle cloth.

Change between a winter and a summer wardrobe.

How?

Wardrobe Empty out the whole wardrobe and start again from scratch. Sort clothes into five piles:

- **Give away** It's best to give away clothes you don't use.

- **Throw away** Broken and discoloured clothes should go straight in the bin.

- **Sell** Sell any nice clothes. Advertise in a paper, or use one of the many online trading sites.

- **Keep** There should only be real favourites in this category, and very little else. Be strict! Ask yourself: Do I wear this? Am I really ever likely to wear it again?

- **Not sure** Favourites you just don't have the heart to get rid of can be placed in a special drawer. If you don't wear them within the next year, it's probably time to get rid of them.

It's much easier to see properly when the wardrobe's empty. Go through the clothes and think about what you really need. Perhaps more hangers, or extra storage boxes for seasonal storage. Wipe the inside of the wardrobe using a miracle cloth and vacuum it before returning the clothes to their rightful place.

Seasonal storage
Gloves, woolly hats and thermal underwear can be put away during the summer. Keep them in labelled boxes. Similarly, put away summer dresses and shoes during the winter.

Utility room

MEMO

- Always empty pockets before putting clothes in the washing machine. Small objects may get stuck and pens may leak.

- Stretch bed linen well, as soon as it's been washed. It will take up far less space in the airing cupboard.

Everyday luxury

Is there anything more practical than a utility room? In fact it's so practical, it's like a touch of luxury. Having all that extra room makes sorting, washing, hanging up, drying and ironing clothes so much easier.

If your washing machine and tumble dryer are in the kitchen or bathroom, you will obviously have less space available, but see it as a challenge – you're bound to be able to come up with a few smart solutions! And as always, it's about getting back to basics: focus on maximising storage and workspace, and avoid nooks and crannies where dust can gather.

Don't forget the lint filter in the tumble dryer!

Always in the utility room

Shelves and cupboards for detergent, fabric softener, clothes pegs and so on.

High legs on the floor cabinets, obviously!

Have a special place for dirty laundry. Large families may need more than one laundry basket. Use one for whites and one for colours, and your laundry will already be sorted when the time comes to do a wash.

Often in the utility room

Wash regularly – once a week is about right. If you wash every other week it becomes a whole day's work – and it will take ages to sort everything.

Take care of your clothes and avoid washing them too often. Thick jumpers and suit jackets generally just need airing a while to freshen them up.

Dust regularly, as there's no end of dust and lint flying around in a utility room. Dust with a damp miracle cloth.

Vacuum the utility room as part of your weekly cleaning routine.

Sometimes in the utility room

Carry out basic maintenance on your washing machine and tumble dryer. Clean the filters and keep the machines clean as well. If you have a condenser dryer, empty the water container regularly.

Descale the iron.

Clean or rinse the floor drain (if your utility is a wetroom).

How?

Sort Divide your laundry into colours and follow the washing instructions on each piece of clothing. Wash whites with whites, colours with colours and black with black. Bear in mind that quite a few things should only be washed at 30°C.

Wash White laundry, bed linen and towels should be washed at the highest temperature possible, ideally 60°C. Colours are generally washed at 40°C.

Don't overfill the washing machine as it may not spin properly. Two-thirds full is about right. Always check zips and buttons before putting the washing in the machine. Do up zips and buttons on trousers. On shirts, blouses and jackets, leave the buttons open but do up any zips.

There are different detergents for white and coloured washing, the difference being that the one for whites contains bleach. Don't use too much detergent. Find out how hard your local water is and follow the dosage instructions on the pack.

Underwire bras and other delicates should be washed in a laundry bag, which saves both the garments and the washing machine.

Dry Shake the clothes while they're still wet to reduce wrinkles. Hang the clothes so they are smooth. Heavy garments should dry flat so as not to lose their shape.

Iron Different fabrics should be ironed at different temperatures. Check the washing instructions. Start by ironing the clothes that require a low temperature. Note that it's easier to iron clothes if they're still a bit damp.

Stains

The secret to stain removal is speed. The quicker you deal with a stain, the more likely you are to remove it. Wash items according to the washing instructions.

When treating stains: Use a concealed hem to first check that the treatment won't affect the garment's colour. Always lay a clean white terry towel or a thick layer of kitchen roll under the stain. This will absorb any loose dirt and stop the stain from running out onto the garment.

Dried-in stains will soften if you leave the garment to soak in water for a few hours. If you like, add a little glycerine as this dissolves dirt. Then, wash the garment using your normal detergent.

Blood Soak immediately in cold water. Then rub a little soft soap onto the fresh stain and wash as normal.

Candle wax Break and pick off as much wax as possible. Put kitchen roll or coffee filter papers on both sides of the stain and press with an iron at the temperature recommended on the washing instructions.

Chewing gum Place the garment in the freezer, then break the chewing gum off once it has frozen.

Chocolate Rub the stain with soft soap, then wash as normal.

Coffee Detergents containing bleach generally remove coffee stains.

Collar stains If the stains remain after machine washing, rub using a bar of soap and machine wash once again.

Fruit and berries Use a detergent containing bleach and wash according to the instructions. If the stain persists, you can buy special stain removers for fruit, berries and wine.

Grass Green grass stains can be treated with soft soap. Rub the stain with the soap and leave for an hour or so, then wash as normal.

Ink Rinse thoroughly under running water. Treat with liquid detergent and rinse once more. If the stain remains, treat it with a solution of equal parts lemon juice and household ammonia. Discard the solution once you've finished.

Milk and cream Pre-treat the stain with liquid detergent or washing-up liquid under running water, then rinse and wash as normal. Ideally, use a detergent containing bleach.

Mud Let the mud dry and then brush off as much as possible. Rub the fabric between your hands and the mud will fall off. Then brush again and wash as normal.

Red wine Pour salt over the stain and leave it for a while to absorb the wine. Soak in cold water and then wash as normal.

Sweat and deodorant stains Rub with a standard white bar of soap, then wash as normal.

Odour Get rid of unpleasant smells from curtains and rag-rugs, for example.

Mix 300 ml of white vinegar (12%) with 10 litres of lukewarm water in a large bowl or bucket and soak the fabric. Soak white and light items for 30 minutes, and dark and coloured items for 15-20 minutes.

A clean planet!

We must take care of our wonderful planet. It's not only our homes that have to be clean, but the world around us.

Sort your rubbish – you can buy excellent waste-sorting bins to make the job easier.

Do not use unnecessarily strong cleaning agents. Try to choose mild alternatives that are biodegradable.

When washing up by hand, put in the plug and fill the sink. Avoid washing up under running water.

Don't wash laundry or dishes unnecessarily. Before starting the washing machine or dishwasher, have another look round for odd socks, cups and glasses.

Clean with a clear conscience.

Starting is half the battle.

Cleaning – It's as easy as 1, 2, 3.... Or is it?

Now you know exactly what to do to get your house nice and clean. There is, of course, the small matter of actually getting round to it! Well, one idea is to be positive – never negative. Begin by visualising your nice clean home in your mind, and come up with a tempting reward – a treat to be enjoyed once you've finished cleaning. Then make yourself a cup of tea of coffee, open the windows wide and put on your favourite music. Now it's just a matter of getting started. Happy cleaning!

Be a doer Has that pile of papers on the desk grown to ridiculous proportions? Have you been looking at it with a sinking heart for several weeks? Half-finished projects and messy piles take up a lot of thinking energy – just by being there. Deal with the problem straight away – it actually doesn't take that long once you get started.

Don't get stuck So you've started having a good clearout, but suddenly find yourself tied up with all kinds of broken or odd things you're not sure what to do with. Have a special storage box for broken stuff you don't know if you want to keep. Put them in the box straight away and go back to them at a later point.

Make lists Don't know where to start? Make a list of everything you want to clean. For instance: Clear out wardrobe, Tidy desk, Defrost freezer. You don't have to do everything in one go. Do one thing at a time and tick them off as you go along.

Reward A clean, tidy home is a reward in itself. But why not treat yourself to a nice dinner, a relaxing bath or your favourite dessert? You deserve it!

For the family

Everyone can help out with the cleaning one way or another. Unnecessary discussions and even arguments can be avoided if everyone does their bit.

Cleaning roster Get together and talk about how you'd each like things to work at home. How much should you clean, and what needs to be included in the weekly cleaning routine? Who should be responsible for what? Writing down each point on a piece of paper is a good idea, rather than trying to keep it all in your head. Once each person knows what they're responsible for, there need never be any discussion. Draw up a permanent cleaning roster, or write a new one each week for variation.

And when you begin your new cleaning routine, remember that old habits die hard. But stick with it. You will begin to see results and after a while you'll realise that cleaning takes less time and energy.

Children

Learn Show children how to clean and make it a family activity. Have fun! Sing and dance. There might even be a small reward at the end…

Neat and tidy Assign everything its own place, and make it a habit always to put things back where you found them. Have a few minutes' tidying-up time every evening, and take the opportunity to chat a little.

Being involved Help each other out with day-to-day things like cooking and clearing the breakfast table.

Encourage Everyone does what they can. For a young child to make their own bed is quite an achievement! Take care to notice these things and remember to praise them.

Cleaning roster

Here is a sample cleaning roster for a whole family. There are specific tasks for every family member – try swapping every other week or so.

Mum

- Do the shopping, cook and wash up.
- Make the bed.
- For the weekly clean: tidy up, wipe and dust.

Dad

- Do the washing, hang clothes up to dry, fold and put away.
- Change the bed.
- For the weekly clean: vacuum and mop the floors.

Children

- Make their bed.
- Clean and vacuum their room.
- Help set the table.
- Take the rubbish out.

Weekly cleaning

Open windows and give your home a good airing. Deal with one room at a time. Follow your checklist and tick things off as you get them done. Remember to start at the top and work down. Finish off by vacuuming all rooms and mopping the most frequently used spaces.

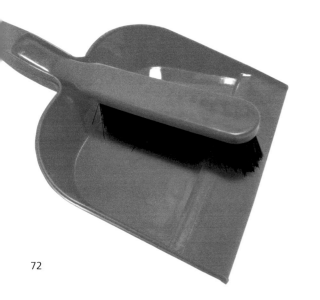

Kitchen

- [ ] Clear the worktops. Wash things up or put them in the dishwasher.
- [ ] Wipe the cooker, sink unit and worktops with a dishcloth. Wipe other surfaces with a miracle cloth and diluted soft soap.
- [ ] Clear old food out of the fridge.
- [ ] Change the tea-towel and hand towel.
- [ ] Empty the rubbish (this should obviously be done more than once a week!).

Bathroom and Utility room

- [ ] Tidy up and throw away empty packaging.
- [ ] Clean the toilet bowl, both inside and out. Remove the seat and rinse it.
- [ ] Clean the wash-basin, bath and shower.
- [ ] Polish the bathroom mirror.
- [ ] Empty the waste bin.
- [ ] Change the towels and make sure there's enough toilet paper.
- [ ] Wash any dirty laundry.
- [ ] Empty the filters/water container on the washing machine and tumble dryer.

Living room and Hallway

- [ ] Tidy up, organise remotes and sort out newspapers and magazines.
- [ ] Puff up the cushions and air any blankets.
- [ ] Dust all surfaces, not forgetting the TV.
- [ ] Tidy up coats and shoes in the hallway.

Bedroom and Workspace

- [ ] Tidy up. Put clean clothes in drawers and wardrobes, dirty clothes in the laundry basket.
- [ ] Tidy the desk.
- [ ] Air the bedclothes. Change bed linen at least every other week.
- [ ] Dust all surfaces, including lamps and computers.
- [ ] Empty waste bins.

Children's room

- [ ] Tidy up the toys.
- [ ] Wash up the toy tea set if there is one.
- [ ] Dust all surfaces.
- [ ] Empty waste bins.

Emergency cleaning

The place is a tip and your guests are about to arrive. What now?! Don't panic, now's the perfect time for a bit of cheating. Think about which rooms the guests will see, and focus on those.

- Open the windows and let in a little air.
- Give the bathroom a quick clean. Give the wash-basin and toilet a wipe, and change the towels.
- Tidy up the shoes and coats in the hallway.
- No time to vacuum – just pick up any big lumps of dust by hand.
- Wipe any crumbs off the kitchen worktops and take out the rubbish.

- Put away anything unnecessary in the living room and puff up the sofa cushions.
- Smooth the bedclothes and put on the bedspread if you have one. If you don't have time, keep the bedroom door closed.

MEMO

Write your own cleaning tips here to make sure you don't forget them.

At last, I've finished tidying! Only now I can't find where I put....

_____

_____

_____

_____

_____

_____

_____

_____

_____

_____

_____

Index